A Temple Looming

A Temple Looming

Poems by Lenard D. Moore

WordTech Editions

Published by WordTech Editions
P.O. Box 541106
Cincinnati, OH 45254-1106

Typeset in Adobe Caslon by WordTech
Commmunications LLC

ISBN: 9781934999103
LCCN: 2008927619

Poetry Editor: Kevin Walzer
Business Editor: Lori Jareo

Visit us on the web at www.wordtechweb.com

Acknowledgments

Grateful acknowledgment is made to the editors of the following journals, where some of the poems in this collection were previously published:

Asheville Poetry Review: "Women in a Photo Album."

Bma: The Sonia Sanchez Literary Review: "Still-Life Woman."

Crab Orchard Review: "At Six O'Clock," "It Begins with Middle Passage."

One Trick Pony: "Rebecca in the Rattan Chair."

Sauti Mpya: "A Contrast Of Two Lives," "Beyond Black," "Using Light," (which is now titled "Elk, Circa 1902").

The Saracen: "The Family."

Windhover: "Another Picture Moment," (which is now section 2 of "No Utopia") "Imagining Peach."

Thanks to The Association to Preserve the Eatonville Community, Inc. for publishing "Frazzled" and "Beyond Black" in the anthology *Metaphors: Poems in the Tradition of Zora Neale Hurston* (2001).

Many of these poems are in debt to the critical eyes

and comments of the Carolina African American Writers' Collective and the Washington Street Writers' Group in Raleigh, North Carolina, from 1995 to 1999. I also greatly appreciate L. Teresa Church, Sally A. Drucker, the late Ellen T. Johnston-Hale (1930-2005), Janice W. Hodges, Opal J. Moore, Jerry W. Ward, Jr., Bruce Lader and Carole Boston Weatherford for their careful reading of individual poems. In addition, I am grateful to Elizabeth Alexander, Al Maginnes, Robin M. Caudell, Karma Mayet Johnson, Gina M. Streaty, Evie Shockley, Toi Derricotte and David Rigsbee for reading this collection of poems in manuscript form. I give thanks to Sally B. Buckner for assisting with arranging these poems in the best possible order for this book. I also give thanks to the late Doris Lucas Laryea (1937-2004) and Everett Hoagland for their encouragement. Furthermore, I am grateful for the support of my wife Lynn Moore and our late daughter Maiisha LaShawn Moore (1982-2004) who listened to me read these poems in various stages of development and offered positive feedback. I am also grateful for the support of my mother Mary Louise Moore and my father Rogers Edward Moore and my brothers and sisters, as they have traveled with me to give these poems life by reading them to audiences.

This book is for the Carolina African American Writers Collective: Oktavi Allison, Kim Arrington, Harold Adrian Beckles, Bennis M. Blue, Victor E. Blue (1968-2002), Beverly Fields Burnette, Sheila Kingsberry Burt, Chezia Thompson Cager, Christian A. Campbell, L. Teresa Church, M'sapa Corley,

DeLana Dameron, Taian T. Davis, Rebecca Lynn Delbridge, Camille T. Dungy, Angela Belcher Epps, Myshalae Jamerson Euring, Estelle Elizabeth Farley, Cherryl Floyd-Miller, Cynthia M. Gary, Ebony Noelle Golden, Mary Stone Hanley, Janice W. Hodges, Sereion S. Humphrey, Brian H. Jackson, Paula White Jackson (1947-2007), Chantal James, Honoree Fanonne Jeffers, Valjeanne Jeffers-Thompson, Candace M. Jenkins, Michelle L. Johnson, Patricia A. Johnson, Diane Judge, Bridgette A. Lacy, Evelyn Lemar, Raina J. Leon, Mendi Lewis-Townsend Obadike, Charles L. Lindsay, Melina Brown Mangal, Nimat Marie, McCrouah, Musette France McKelvey, Gaye L. Newton, Keith Obadike, Grace Cloris Ocasio, Tanisha Ottley, Wendell W. Ottley III, Ajene Quillin, Barbara Lucas Ross, Nancy Shakir, Odessa Shaw, Jr., Evie Shockley, Christopher Stanard, Vickie T. Stanford, Darrell D. Stover, Gina M. Streaty, Eleanora E. Tate, Roma Turner, Afefe L. Tyehimba (formerly known as Lana C. Williams), Karen Wade, Jacqueline D. Washington, Carole Boston Weatherford, Elizabeth Wellington, Sandra L. West and Jackiann Wilson.

Thanks also to Lori Jareo and Kevin Walzer of WordTech Editions for their support of this book.

Contents

Part I

An Album of Strong Old Men

JEREMIAH

He peers out small eyes, ogling,
hunkers in white shirt and tie.
His homemade gray suit coat hugs tight.

Against the light,
his wide face is clean,
follicles empty.

Lines on his forehead
are two rivers reeling parallel,
eyebrows bank slightly.

His lips stay sealed
like a widow in deep pain,
against a story.

GIDEON

He has left his image on paper,
gone into permanence,
white bristles rising from his head.

The light dazzles,
heightens one cheek
like bleach in a whirlpool.

He looks straight ahead
with his eyes dreaming,
and above his upper lip

thick mustache
a line of black chalk
on brown paper.

MOSES

Frownless forehead,
no smile escapes
his too tight mouth.

Huge white collar flipped down
stiff on peppermint-striped shirt,
bright as any firefly's glow.

In the dark tube of his throat,
his stories of family, framing ancestors,
remain hushed, soft wind.

He looks slantwise:
Moses, mentor man, preacher.
Moses, original, black dreamer.

Elk, Circa 1902

Strong is the man, standing,
knees kept straight
in sharp-creased pants.
Where he stands a line of light
falls into the growing silence.
Medallions pinned
on the uniform. Sash drapes
over his shoulder.
Wide belt around his waist,
brass buckle shining like sunglow,
and a sword hangs from his hip.
White-gloved, his hands hang open,
massive, against the coat.
Crowning his head
a hat,
white plumes
reaching sunflowers.

The Soldier

The photograph's subject now aged
through time's ripening; decades later
the background gray,
a dream.

Splendid in uniform,
the barrel-straight stare
of his pure black face
shines like a bullet.

Imagine he'd not returned
from the Great War,
leaving a void in his family,
and in this picture.

Beyond Black

Black goes beyond your shaven jaw,
your tweed coat,

the twisted tie.

Scarred valleys furrow your face.
Reflected in your eyes,

the lynchings of the twenties.

Why are you alone?
The possibilities go

beyond this photograph.

This Black Man

The black felt hat trimmed with wide ribbon
cools on his left leg.
His tight tweed coat is fastened
over yoke of his white shirt and thin tie.
He waits, sheened as a leaf.

A Contrast of Two Lives

Albert looks like my next-door cousin,
who used to smack a baseball
clean out the park.
Unlike my uniformed cousin,
Albert wears a doublebreasted suit.
Head trimmed closely,
his eyes glitter
as if kin stamped pride
in them.
My cousin's roots
spread through earth
in our blooming hometown,
but Albert waits branchless
in a browning field.

Mister Man

Mister man,
you sit sideways,
head tilted down
telling the photographer
your story before
flash blights
your simple eye.
A pocket watch hangs
from lapel to breast pocket
on your solid black suit.
White is the starched-stiff shirt
beneath your chin,
a foil for your necktie.
Your hands, wide and dark
press against your knees.
No one frames you.
No one appears to see
the broad nose, wide mouth, crew cut
in the thick plot of hair.
What you do not say
and any talk of joy,
is postponed
in the pupils of your eyes.

No Utopia

1

In front of unknown trees
and a mountain, all's steady,
near the vanishing point,

an ashen girl, five years old,
stares earthward into a breeze.
Draped from her neck,

a white sweater conceals spindly arms.
Plaits hang down the side of her face,
her forehead protrudes.

2

In the back room
of the old building,
he leans forward
toward the iron machine,
polishing a broad shoe, black,
Custom Oak stamped on its sole.

He presses the tip of the shoe
against the rotating buffer.
His head, gray and stiff, casts
a shadow on the pallid wall
above jars of polish.

His fingers, long and thick
and strong, tell the story.
Where he stands now

in simple smock,
auctioned men stood in single file.

Man

the way
your mouth
clenches
makes me wonder

what words
could unfurl
resonate
stern steel
without end

everything else
remains hushed
and knotted
like the tie
around your white shirt
that you wear
like scarless skin

my memory
reunwinds
to a similar frame
my grandfather groomed
when I was
somewhere in boyhood

Part II

Women in a Photo Album

1. *Nola*

The woman arced her lips,
a prolonged unhurtful hush
when the slave's story unfolds,

though she might spill daggers,
since she knows the blood
binding ancestors everywhere.

I think this woman spoke to me
one night when lightning flashed her face,
high cheekbones alluring

like the lens of her glasses
or her hanging black curls
or the cross around her neck.

This wise woman leaned over me
and lanced the darkness
with flame-like words.

She still slips into my room;
here and there words flare.
There is no single explanation.

2. *Kizzie And Lizzie*

Two women stand
against a simple backdrop.
Hair slicked down,

they stare sorrow out
to the bone
so bleak others feel it.

The women look like twins
--same cotton dress
adorn their thick bodies

in front of a wooden post
past the benches
in the back of the room.

These are women
with stories swelling their bellies
when language is mute

as ashes in the wind
or dust hanging in the air
passing slowly over earth.

3. *Ellen*

Low v-neck dress, the woman,
with plump dimpled cheeks, strikes a pose
plain as the clouds overhead.

White pearls rope her neck,
bloom solo at her ears.
Her face frames sadness.

Her skin etched charcoal
heated gray like coal in an iron stove
where whatever burns flakes into itself.

Her broad shoulders slightly slanted,
head leaning forward,
the silence she keeps.

Framed

The woman
in the photo
looks like Aunt Muriel:
fair-skinned, thin nose,
full lips, broad brows,
flat forehead, and hair
long on both sides
but curled at its ends.
Her poised body,
so full
of pride in a house-cleaning world,
wears a checkered cotton dress
the way Aunt Muriel did.
The scene is somber:
she is so square
to the camera,
just right
in time's lilac deepening
for claiming kin
nearly forgotten.

Evalene

I like the way you sit:
sideways, legs crossed,
cotton skirt tight
below knobby knees,
left hand on
the higher knee,
and right hand on
the chair's round back.

I like the way you pose:
twisted around
on the chair, without words;
stiff, head tilted
towards the left shoulder;
no lines, no circles
below the eyes.

I like the way you wait:
wearing a straw hat
ringed with white flowers
like it ain't nobody's business;
lips glossed and puckered
as if they were fixed for a kiss;
white shirt, matching jacket,
sweet baby, as if you were kin to me.

Woman Waiting on a Park Bench

Her lips, a full black plum,
invite me
into a warm bond.
She pours the light
on me: knows
how Eve bit the fruit
hanging perfect in Eden.
Like Adam, I believe
in woman.
If I could, I would clutch
her hands as they glow
in the sunrise.
I want to hold,
comfort her,
shed secrets like skin.

The Speaking Face of Delilah

Struggle was my life, mixed blood.
I stayed simple on southern soil.

I bent low in countless cotton fields,
back ached like a tooth gone bad.

"Let's leave," I whispered to my mother.
She stopped and clutched my hand, speechless.

Woman

the light strikes
your profile
rekindles
my spirit
as full as
the rose
pinned over
your bloomed breasts

sitting on the bed
listening to Billie Holiday
sing "Body And Soul"
while clutching
this photograph
in the middle
of warm night
i am awestruck

Closed Road to Uncertainties

Caught up in a snapshot
a stale solemnness.

Long white table-cloth scarf
wrapped around this woman's neck.

Her eyes could be peas
staring from a big black pot.

Nose studded like a shoe;
mouth shut, a closed road to uncertainties.

She seems as if she is trying to weep,
defining what matters and doesn't.

Turn of the Twentieth Century

She resembles a hometown friend:
big eyes, wide nose, long neck,
and waves of black hair.
Sitting in the backless chair,
she clutches her own wrist.
Her full face is a slate,
telling nothing,
waiting like a tongue.
Against a backdrop of half-light
her skin, black,
without wrinkles, still shines.

Double Exposure

Are you a twin?
Or is this a photographer's trick?

Mysterious woman in twos,
side by side,

your magic profile
glances off,

jolts stillness,
an aching to know

where you've lived—
even your wordless lips

drive me into thick longing
to rescue you

lurching in this room
until you teach me what it means

to float away
into winter's wicked lens.

Emma's Grief

Nearing twilight,
the light-skinned woman looks downward.

She does not
focus on anything.

Lines slant from her nose
through her plump cheeks,
stop just above the corners
of her woman-wide mouth.

The lenses are perfect circles,
O's her eyes peer through.

Her hair is curly, fluffy,
a dark mass,
which shows no gray.

Imagining Peach

too sweet and too juicy
for thin lips to savor

skin too thin and smooth
for stroking by brute fingers

eyes too brown and brilliant
for a man to witness himself held still

hair too long and silky
for bonnet or felt to crown it

small white beads cling
like a shadow around her neck

a flowered lace-trim dress
reveals broad brown shoulders

gloved hands clasp
a blessing

her human heart beats the syllables
of a soon-to-be husband's name

Consider

Big bones, full face, large lips, healthy hair
black as just-tilled earth. The spaced beads

cling to your fleshy collarbone
above the elegant v-neck dress.

Consider, Too

The shadow of smoke
etches itself ashen

so clearly it almost becomes backdrop,
in this photograph that gives grace

the way ordinary things, in sure pose,
fade, hold simple beauty.

Frazzled

The woman's head bends down. She does not look
well; her lips are stuck shut with sadness,
a dream displaced. Her brows are curved like hooks.
It seems the day assaults her too. Her hand
is shiny, poised on bony knee, sweating
those gloomy times. The raving rage inside
her long frail frame inflicted an awful sting.
She sits on broken bench, maybe to confess.
Her velvet dress resembles hand-me-downs
as she sits on the bench; her hair a mess.
No man can wipe away that bluesy frown;
her eyes, barren, express the story best.

Still-Life Woman

Black and white photograph:
a light-skinned woman wears
a short-sleeved, white blouse

tailored with tucks that look like corrugation:
horizontal on the collar, vertical on
the front, and slanting on the sleeves.

Black bow tied around her neck,
though the tail-ribbons hang
between breasts to stomach.

Her blouse is smooth, breasts
totally flat, failed flesh,
frail in their fruitfulness.

No rouge on her full face.
No paint on her pressed lips.
No necklace gleaming on her brawny neck.

She sits in an empty background,
glassy-eyed, entirely plain
and stirred as hair in gusty wind.

Her torso suggests she's tall
as Maya Angelou, an endless stream
of woman, long limbs stilled in time.

The Photographer's Daughter

You show off
your sideways stance.
The background
empty as sky,
your face full of secrets.
The room gray,
your hair wrapped
into a black bun.
The heavy wool coat
keeps your stories warm
inside you.
What words can account
for the yearning I have
to hear you tell about
your hidden self,
the life that might not be
so perfectly posed?
Even if the charm is
in my mind
I still adore your
eyes as if
in a locket.

Miss Woman

Miss woman,
eyes spying me,
as if you knew I'd one day
explore your face
blossomed black and blotchless.
The low-neck dress,
floral,
somehow has meaning.
Black is
the banked-bloomed bun
just back
of your forehead.
A pool of pure light
glitters your skin.
The shadowed background
blends with everything
else, somehow drifts
into the next life.

Butterflies

Young woman, back bow tied
on your gingham dress
like unmoving wings.
You bend slightly
over a much older woman,
right hand holding a book open.

Old woman's left hand keeps
the other side of the book
as flat as the spine allows.
She sits upright, head
tilted forward, eyeglasses glaring
in the book's direction.

You don't look
when silence gives way
to the words that float
from the page,
almost white, lifting splendor
toward the light.

A Temple Looming

Look straight into the lens
that caught you,

stand as the still-light goes white;
no one else recognizes the vacant stare

of your too-dark eyes
like chinquapins.

Fur wraps your broad brown shoulders,
velvet hat covers your head

as though it were a bell
waiting to peal at the right moment;

your earrings hang like clappers,
ready to swing.

In front of a wrought iron gate
you stand, slim and solemn,

a temple looming in light,
and while your mouth stays shut

like a window, words themselves
lock in the throat.

Part III

It Begins with Middle Passage

The way the children are
becoming who they are reveals
their story is deeper than skin:
the older boy stands soldier straight
in a sailor's uniform, then too,
his head's clean shaven;
the younger boy sits stock-still
beside their sister on a chair;
and he's in knickers
and a matching jacket,
ears large as his brother's,
though a shade lighter;
their sister, colorless and plump,
about one-year-old, mouth partly opened,
reclines.
Her hair, ear-length and straight
as pine needles,
but curled at its fine ends.
She's in a dress, sweater, and shoes—
all white in their coverings.
Yet she's not white, but surely mixed
with something that went down
with her mother. This baby girl's
oldest brother is coal black. Blood
remains rich in the children like wet words,
links them still like some small seeds
released in the dark.
How the children form a triangle,
completely in light.

About the Sharecropper's Son

The sheet of sky is coal.
Burn its edges: a curtain
of charcoal
stains the backdrop
with failed light.

Sharecropper's son in a land
of circumstance looks away,
strains for history,
becomes the subject;
story survives.

The round-framed-lens clearly sees
what narrates itself:
spirits surfacing in black and white.
His hairline recedes like a wave
into the river, stopping at a slope.

The Team

See how they sit:
teenaged girls,
legs crossed,
scissors stilled;
four girls gripping ankles
as their bottoms rest
on earth.
Five girls stand
behind them,
one holding a ball
the size of a cantaloupe.
They wear white pullover
shirts, black baggy pants,
black boots, scarves knotted
around their necks.
Behind the team of girls,
trees, pine trees,
the size of telephone poles,
keep still.
The sky, sun sky
drops light
on their human shapes,
the teenaged girls
watch and listen.
The girls'
competing instinct
measures the playing field
that is not there.

Innocence

Two girls and a boy bending their heads
while gazing at a picture book,
and hone childhood days upon their beds,
the times so cheerful—yield a sound outlook.
With white strips of ribbon wrapped round
their heads, the girls earnestly bound
to absorb knowledge their kin must know.
The boy gazes—as if through a window,
thick-carpet hair on his small crown.
Their faces happy, so round and brown.
Their unselfish lives without blues,
hands unstained by paying dues.

Rebecca in the Rattan Chair

I.

The gap-tooth man tore the thin skin of her virginity.
She did not push him away nor did she scream.

Her mother sat her for this picture,
not knowing what he'd done.

The mother only imagined her child was innocent
and saw this man for the first time.

The actual tear that the child denied,
scarred her face.

In her white dress,
she waited like a dreamsitter at midday.

Her mother told her
not to gap her legs.

II.

Rebecca's hair is fine thread,
rooted, where the round hat touches.

Her eyes, polished onyx
in narrow sockets.

Her face, silhouetted,
an elongated summoning.

Her breasts, flat seeds

beneath a shin-length dress.

Her hands, clenched
against her lap.

Her feet, white-shoed,
thin ankles crossed.

At Six O'Clock

Never mind four black boys are grouped closely
in the picture, a curveless row of them.
What matters is they are posing because
they want to. They are unlike evening news.
No two-toned cars skid around the corner.
No handcuffs click. And no bludgeons rising
into the air. These four black boys are like
the ones in my hometown, my neighborhood,
whose tempers never explode like land mines.
They all aim their eyes into the future,
looking content in unmatching suit coats,
these brothers who no longer play in sand.

Cotton Pickers, Circa 1905

Mother and father
occupy twin chairs,
milk-breath daughter
and tall shiny son
stand behind them.
Age fades the room,
family faces loom light
like cottonfields
that crack their backs,
leather their hands.
They shuffled like mules
from plant to plant.
Four faces glisten,
empty eyes,
nothing can change
this family's
lack of smiles.
But divining palms
wait for Sundays.
At night
the moon charts
wells under eyes;
stars, full of prayers, mend.
In that slow uplift of spirits
this worn family is one.

Generations

A family of four poses,
close enough to keep out light,
two girls, little, wholly thin.

Mother smiles, child in lap,
rests chin on daughter's head
is unearthly, could praise and sing
until notes, one by one, burst plum red.

Father has his right hand on other girl's shoulder.
She leans against her sister whose hands are clasped.
Mother leans toward her husband, could take wing.

The man tilts toward his wife,
not fully touching; yet, a gleam
in their eyes baits and burns out strife.

The Old Sycamore's Limbs

hang over the one-lane road I walk.
Leaves lie scattered,
wind stirred.
Over the rise
across the lane:
a stand of longleaf pine,
spaced just enough to hold ghosts
behind an uneven fence.

Up the road, morning light
whitewashes everything,
creates a brilliant tunnel.
I wonder if the road remains
a bed for autumn-brown leaves
on the daystar's other side.

No animals,
no houses between the pines.
Mist settles everywhere.
Only the sycamore is old enough
to know what might have been.
How its curved arms scratch
the bright blue sheet of sky,
wait for whatever spirit comes
to enter its dark rings.

Motherhood

In the glossy oak chair a baby
held by its lovely mother

looks toward the unseen floor,
the mother toward the girl.

Gray envelops the brown pair
like dusk without fireflies' blink.

Entirely Ethereal

only a dark hush
slips from blissful mother
her children look on
a white bow flutters open
in the oldest girl's coarse hair

Abandoned Farm

Doorless in daylight,
it teeters on a frosty plot
gone brown.
No lid covers
the deep hole
in the earth.

The people
who built the outhouse
cared
how sloped,
how far the outhouse was
from the plankhouse,

stamped
this earth
as shadows blackened the base
of the outhouse
twice the size of a phone booth.
No voice rises in the air.

A column of shut barns
leans
like boxes sealing old memories,
closed coffins desiccate
on shadow-struck acres,
left to leafless trees.

Dawn

Daystar floats
into purple cloud pockets
across birdless sky.
Outlines of trees
rise shadowy in the background.
The light looks so small and lonely
in a sky that vast,
turns bloody
when woods wake.

Notes

1. These poems are based on old black and
    white photographs. They were written in
    response to a 1995 request from the visual
    artist Sherman Jenkins to work on an
    interdisciplinary project for two years (1995-
    1997).

2. Early poems from this collection were read
    on Sunday, November 19, 1995, at the City
    Gallery of Contemporary Art, 220 South
    Blount Street, Raleigh, North Carolina.
    LaJan Productions, Inc. in conjunction with
    Vortex Arts presented the (4:00 p.m. to 6:00
    p.m.) program as a Multimedia Visual and
    Performative Production. The literary artists
    who participated were Janice Hodges, Lenard
    Moore, David Prince and Lana Williams.
    The visual artists who participated were
    Barbara Gault, Sherman Jenkins, Rodney
    Lutes and Eric McRay. Each poet was paired
    up with a visual artist and wrote about the
    artwork, including sculptures, photographs,
    and paintings.

3. "Another Picture Moment" (which is now
    section 2 of "No Utopia") and "Imagining
    Peach" were on exhibit from April 27, 1998
    to June 26, 1998, in the 1998 *Windhover*
    Fourth Annual Exhibition, at The Crafts
    Center, North Carolina State University.

LENARD D. MOORE was born in Jacksonville, North Carolina. After graduating from high school and attending two years of college at Coastal Carolina Community College, he enlisted in the U.S. Army and had basic training at Fort Jackson in South Carolina. He later earned a B.A. (Magna Cum Laude) from Shaw University, and an M.A. in English and African American Literature from North Carolina A&T State University.

Moore is a former Writer-in-Residence for the United Arts Council of Raleigh and Wake County. He is the founder and executive director of the Carolina African American Writers' Collective and co-founder of the Washington Street Writers Group. He is President of the Haiku Society of America. He is the 2007-2008 Eastern North Carolina Gilbert-Chappell Distinguished Poet. He is the founding editor of *The CAAWC Newsletter*. He also is the executive chairman of the North Carolina Haiku Society. Moore has taught at Enloe High School, North Carolina A&T State University (Greensboro), North Carolina State University (Raleigh) and Shaw University, and now teaches at Mount Olive College, where he is an Assistant Professor of English and directs the MOC Literary Festival and advises *The Trojan Voices* (formerly known as *The Olive Branch*), the MOC literary journal. He also teaches poetry workshops in the public schools. He is the author of *Desert Storm: A Brief History* (1993), *Forever Home* (1992), and *The Open Eye* (1985). His poems have appeared in more than forty anthologies including *The Garden Thrives* (HarperCollins), *Trouble The Water* (Mentor Books), and *The Haiku Anthology* (Norton), and in the *African American Review, Agni, Callaloo, Essence, The Midwest Quarterly, North Carolina Literary Review, Obsidian II, Poetry Canada Review, Black Arts Quarterly, Pembroke Magazine, Crab Orchard Review, Natural Bridge: A Journal of Contemporary Literature,* and many other magazines. He has also had his essays and book reviews published in *North Dakota Quarterly, Colorado Review, The News & Observer, St. Louis Post-Dispatch, The Pilot, Independent Weekly,* and *Black Issues Book Review*.

In 1996, Moore was awarded the Indies Arts Award. In 1997, he was awarded the Margaret Walker Creative Writing Award for poetry (College Language Association). In 1998, he was selected a Cave Canem Fellow for three years. In 1998, he was also awarded the Tar Heel of The Week Award. In 2006, he was awarded the Sam Ragan Fine Arts Award. He has also been nominated twice for the prestigious Pushcart Prize. In 2007, he was one of the three local organizers for the Haiku North America (HNA) 2007 Conference. He was also the publicity director of the Haiku North America (HNA) 2007 Conference. He lives with his wife in Raleigh, North Carolina.

Printed in the United States
135270LV00002B/1/P

9 781934 999103